Presented to

_____

By _____

Date _____

A World Is Born

*Bible Stories in
Rhythm and Rhyme*

Written by **Sheri Dunham Haan**

Illustrated by **Dan Hochstatter**

8.95

Contents

Preface

Although rhythm and stories both date back almost farther in history than we can trace, very few such stories are based on the Bible. And even fewer have been written down for young children to enjoy.

Nursery age children will probably enjoy the stories most by hearing them read. Soon children begin clapping hands or tapping feet while they listen to the strong cadence. Older children will want to do more complicated clapping rhythms. A family with young children can use these stories effectively as devotions.

Read these stories at a pace that is comfortable for you. As you become more familiar with them, you and your child will enjoy a quick, lively pace. Read a line and have your child chant it back to you. Use the stories as a happy, natural way to reinforce Bible truths.

A World Is Born

—*Genesis 1–2*

Our great and mighty Father
Made this world so long ago.
He did it all quite easily—
He spoke and it was so!

God commanded light to form
To fill the empty space.
Then he called for day and night
To take their proper place.

God called aloud for water.
He called aloud for land.
Brooks and streams and lakes appeared,
And rocks and hills and sand.

Then God called for sky lights!
The stars, the sun, and moon.
And at that moment time began—
Morning, night, and noon.

God soon filled the lakes and land
With lively fish and birds.
What a gorgeous world he'd made
By merely speaking words!

Then God made the animals
All dressed in hairy skins.
At last he made two people
To sing in praise to him!

Called By God
—1 Samuel 3

Hannah had a little boy,
Her heart was filled with thanks and joy;
She named him Samuel.

Hannah brought her son to work
For Eli as a temple clerk
Then left her Samuel.

Now things were pretty bad those days
The people sinned in many ways;
Yet, God liked Samuel.

One night while Samuel slept in bed
A voice spoke out and clearly said,
"Samuel . . . Oh, Samuel."

Samuel ran to Eli's bed

But Eli raised his head and said,

"Lay down, my Samuel."

Again the voice was clearly heard.
It spoke out loud the same few words,
"Samuel . . . Oh, Samuel."

When Samuel ran to Eli's bed
Eli knew and quickly said,
"It's God's voice, Samuel."

921988

Samuel went to bed once more
God's voice called out just as before,
"Samuel . . . Oh, Samuel."

Samuel answered, "Speak to me.
Your servant, Lord, I'll always be.
I am your Samuel."

God spoke about the things he'd do
And said to Samuel, "I choose you
To be my prophet, Samuel."

The Scheming Plan
That Failed
—*Daniel 6*

Darius had some chosen men
Who helped him rule his land,
And yet the king chose Daniel
As his best and favorite man.

The other men were jealous,
They schemed a tricky plan;
They asked the king to make a law
And sign it with his hand.

The law commanded everyone
All ladies and all men
To worship only Darius
Or fear the lions' den!

Yet every morning, noon, and night
Daniel prayed with thanks,
The sneaky men were watching
And caught him by their prank.

Daniel then was thrown before
The hungry lion beasts,
But God made absolutely sure
They could not eat their feast!

And when the king discovered
That God had such great power,
He vowed his land would serve the Lord
Beginning at that hour!
Yes!
Beginning at that hour!

A Gigantic Catch

—Luke 5:4-11

Peter was a fisherman
Who'd spent a useless night,
He'd fished with all his buddies
But there were no fish in sight!

Then Jesus came to join the men
Quite early the next day.
So many folks had followed him—
He hoped to get away.

"Say, Peter," Jesus called aloud,
"Row out a little way!
There are so many fish out there
That you will be amazed!"

"Oh, no, dear Master," Peter sighed,
"That's just where we have been!
But if you say the fish are there
We'll try it once again."

So Peter did as Jesus said
And dropped his nets down deep.
At once his nets were filled with fish—
More fish than he could keep!

And at that moment Peter saw
The Lord's great power again;
"From now on, Peter," Jesus said,
"You'll always fish for men!"
"Yes!"
"You'll always fish for men!"

A Brand New Man

—*Luke 19:1-9*

Zacchaeus was a little man—
Well known throughout the land.
He cheated extra taxes
Out of every farmer's hand.

Then Jesus came to Jericho,
And as he traveled through—
Zacchaeus climbed into a tree
To get a perfect view.

Jesus stopped and spoke to him,
"Zacchaeus, you come down."
Zacchaeus was astounded so
He scrambled to the ground.

Jesus then went on to say,
"I'm coming to your home."
Zacchaeus was so honored
That his eyes and face just shone!

The longer Jesus talked to him
Zacchaeus saw his need,
He knew he was a sinner
And he wanted to be freed!

Zaccheus truly met the Lord
Who washed his sins away.
Zaccheus' heart was clean and fresh
Beginning on that day!

Home Again
—Luke 24:44-53

Jesus' work was finished.
He'd died at Calvary,
He'd come to earth to give his life
For folks like you and me.

Then he had arisen,
He left that lonely tomb;
He knew that he'd be leaving
For heaven very soon.

He took his dear disciples
Up to a mountain top,
He told them that he'd leave them
But his love would never stop.

"Bring the news to everyone,
Explain just why I've come;
Tell all that they can live in joy
If they believe God's Son."

Then Jesus turned to bless them,
He held his hands up high;
And as he did, he left them—
He rose into the sky.

Because of what had happened
The disciples were amazed,
Their hearts were filled
                with so much joy
They prayed and sang in praise!

Stories I liked best of all